My First ABCs

for the college-bound infant

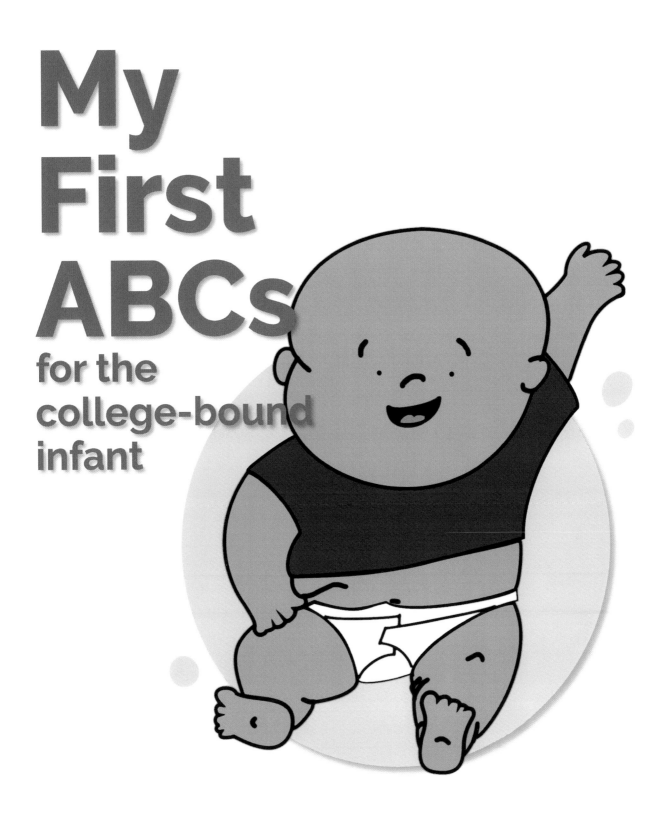

freyin publications
New York + Shanghai + San Francisco

Dedicated to all the

neurotic parents

who dream of getting their kid(s) into

Harvard

before they're even born.

Oh, you're not *neurotic*?

Not even a **little bit**?

Aa

Anthropophagy

Cannabalism

Brobdingnagian

Gigantic

Chaetophorous

In need of a shave

Putting
one's foot in
one's mouth

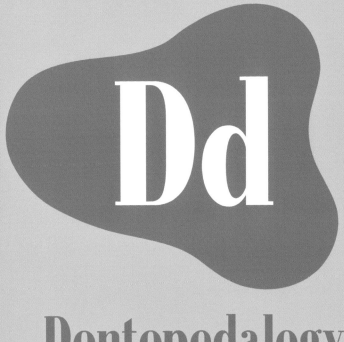

Dd

Dontopedalogy

Eellogofusciou-
hipoppokunurious

Floccinaucinihilipilification

Setting at little or no value

GALACTOPHAGIST

Milk
Drinker

Hippopotomonstrosesquippedaliophobia

Poisoning
resulting from
a wound
inflicted
by a
venomous
fish

Ichthyoacanthotoxism

Jettatura

A curse of the evil eye

Easily recognizable

KENSPECKLE

Leiotrichous

Having straight, smooth hair

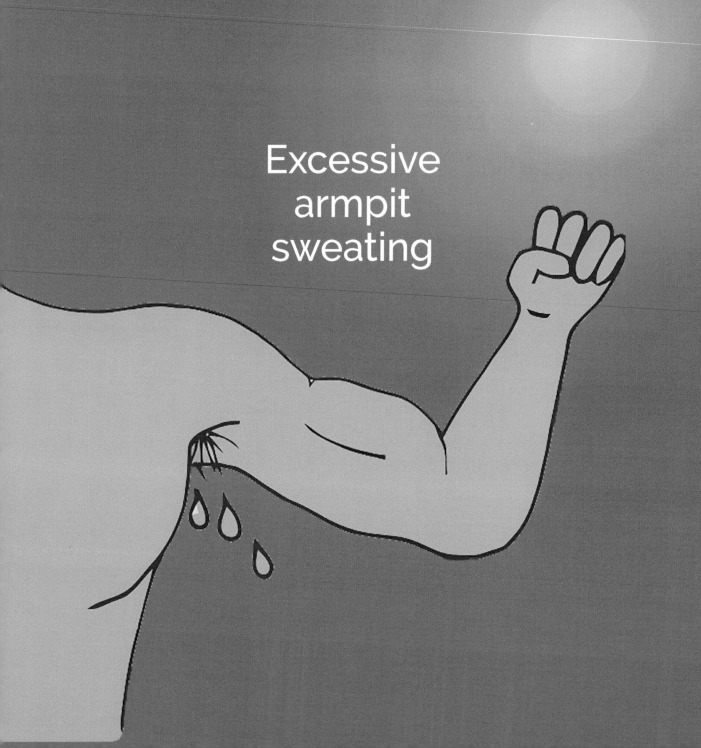

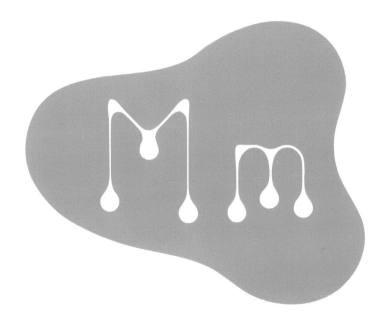

Maschalephidrosis

Nephelococcygia

Act of finding shapes in the clouds

Lighthouse

Obeliscolychny

PANANADENTATE

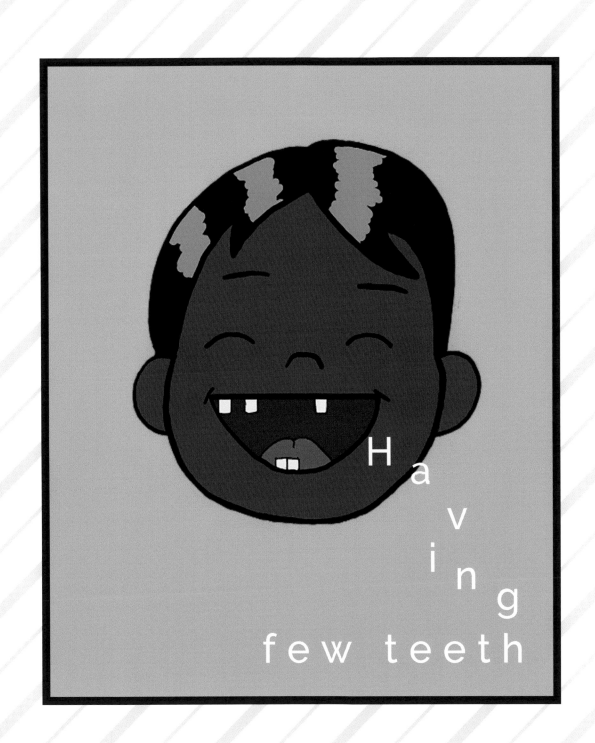

Having few teeth

An arrangement of five things
in a square or rectangle

with one at each corner and
one in the middle

Quincunx

Raiment

Clothing, garments

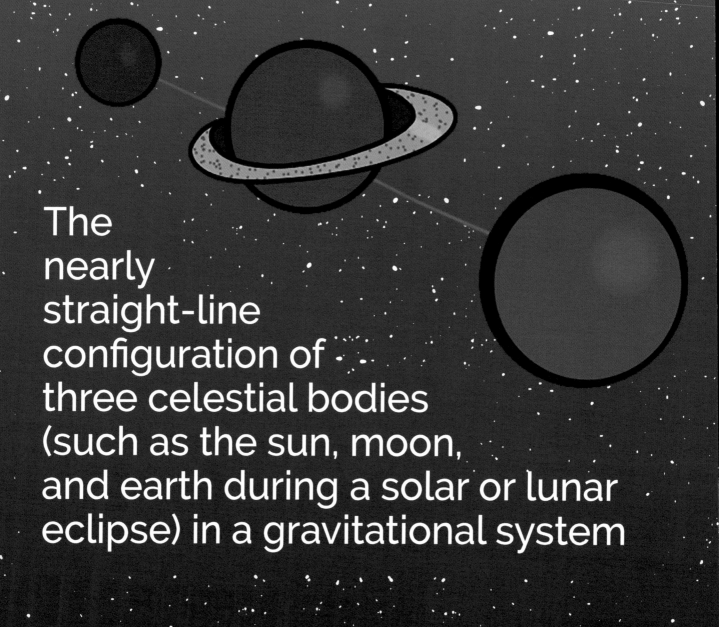

The
nearly
straight-line
configuration of
three celestial bodies
(such as the sun, moon,
and earth during a solar or lunar
eclipse) in a gravitational system

Syzygy

Tintinnabulation

The ringing or
sounding of bells

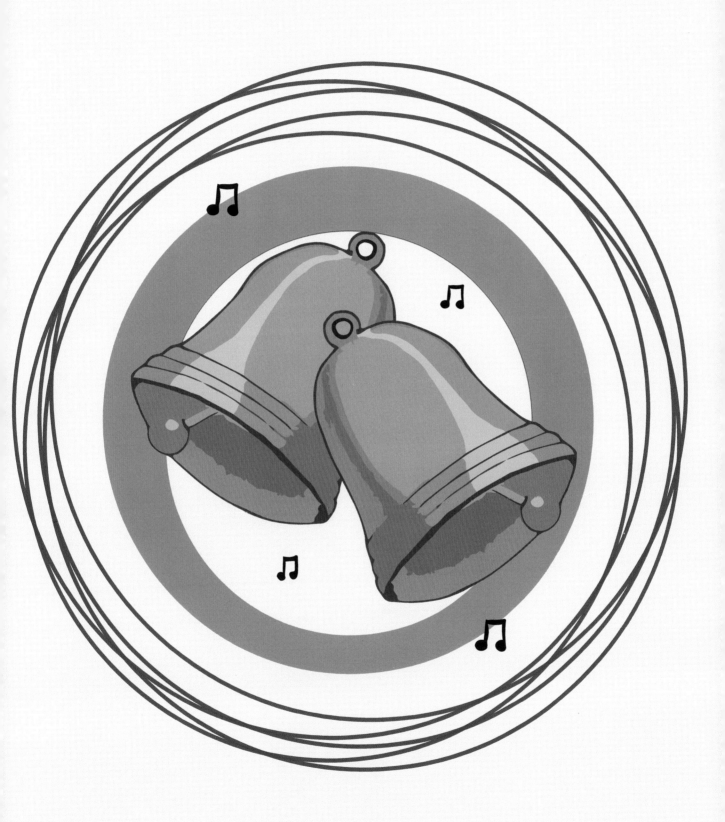

Umbrella shaped

Uu

Umbraculiform

Vocables

Words composed of various
sounds or letters
without regard to their meaning

To feel nausea

The lore of hotels and inns

XENODOCHEIONOLOGY

YANGOCHIROPTERA

Microbat

Zenzizenzizenzic

Eighth power of a number

Anthropophagy – Cannibalism. *Please don't eat my 1000 IQ baby!*

Brobdingnagian – Of huge size; gigantic; tremendous. *May I have a brobdingnagian ice cream sundae please? See? Correct grammar and an ice cream sundae. It's a win-win.*

Chaetophorous – Bristly, or in need of a shave. *Kind of like first-time dads who have no idea what they're doing.*

Dontopedalogy - Putting one's foot in one's mouth (figuratively). *Ew! That's gross. Oh ok, it's figurative. Never mind.*

Eellogofusciouhipoppokunurious - Good. *A waste of both time and space, because this word will never in a million years show up on the SATs, which is also good. The part about the SATs.*

Floccinaucinihilipilification - Setting at little or no value. *If your kid ever has dreams of starting a lemonade stand, tell them not to do this.*

Galactophagist - Milk drinker. *Come to mama!*

Hippopotomonstrosesquippedaliophobia - Fear of long words. *What kind of monster would do that to those poor people with hippopotomonstrosesquippedaliophobia?*

Ichthyoacanthotoxism - Poisoning resulting from a wound inflicted by a venomous fish. *Parenting 101 is to avoid that.*

Jettatura - A curse of the evil eye. *However, an evil eye pendant can protect you from the evil eye curse. If you're not following, look it up.*

Kenspeckle - Easily recognizable. *I bet you didn't recognize Mikhail Gorbachev. If you did, you get a gold star! Congratulations!*

Leiotrichous - Having straight smooth hair. *Oh, it's so shiny! What hair products do you use? Can I touch it?*

Maschalephidrosis - Excessive armpit sweating. *Is this book making you apprehensive? So many long, unfamiliar, daunting words. Oh, it's not? All right then.*

Nephelococcygia - Act of finding shapes in clouds. *Ooh! That one looks like a jettatura! And that one's a galactophagist!*

Obeliscolychny - Lighthouse. *A house of enlightenment, one that illuminates the path to success. Or just a tower for the boats.*

Paucidentate - Having few teeth. *Like your small child, who hopefully has teeth growing in. It'd be a problem if they were already falling out.*

Quincunx - An arrangement of five things in a square or rectangle with one at each corner and one in the middle (like the number 5 on dice). *I challenge you to challenge your kid to arrange something in a quincunx. To test if they were actually listening, you know?*

Raiment - Clothing, garments. *Also those onesies, unicorn pajamas, and all those things you put on yourself to keep people from staring when you go outside.*

Syzygy - The nearly straight-line configuration of three celestial bodies (such as the sun, moon, and earth during a solar or lunar eclipse) in a gravitational system. *Such a fun word for a kind of dull definition. It's really a shame, since you'll never have those competitions where you try to say "syzygy" ten times fast. Wait, no one ever wanted one of those? Well, your loss, I guess.*

Tintinnabulation - The ringing or sounding of bells. *Ding dong! Who's there! No one? Aw man, a ding dong ditch!*

Umbraculiform - Botany umbrella-shaped. *Just in case someone wants to go into botany or something like that. Gotta have something for everyone, right?*

Vocables - Words composed of various sounds or letters without regard to its meaning. *Like scat, which has an extremely unfortunate name. Da dee do da, we can just ignore that-ah.*

Wamble - To feel nausea. *Let me tell you, some of these words are so long and complicated you feel nausea just looking at them. Are you in the same boat? Post a comment down below. Ha! Gotcha! We don't have a down below!*

Xenodocheionology - The lore of hotels and inns. *I got no comments. It's cool, and um, yeah, that's it.*

Yangochiroptera - Microbat (classification of bat). *For all those budding biologists out there, better start studying this one!*

Zenzizenzizenzic - Eighth power of a number. *I bet if you use that in a math class, no one's going to have any idea what you're talking about, even the teacher. Better hire a new one then, yeah? Kidding*

Merriam-Webster: *Anthropophagy, Ichthyaocanthotoxism, Leiotrichous, Quincunx, Raiment, Syzygy, Tintinnabulation, Vocables, Wamble, Xenodocheionology*

Collins: *Brobdingnagian, Jettatura, Umbraculiform*

Phrontistery: *Chaetophorus, Dontopedalogy, Eellogofusciouhipoppokunurious, Floccinaucinihilipilification, Galactophagist, Maschalephidrosis, Nephelococcygia, Obeliscolychny, Zenzizenzizenzic*

Healthline: *Hippopotomonstrosesquippedaliophobia*

Oxford: *Kenspeckle*

Lexico by Oxford: *Paucidentate*

Wikipedia: *Yangochiroptera*

A dedication to all new parents

Relax, have fun, and take one day at a time
This book is what happens when you do.

When our Ivy League sweatshirt-wearing neighbors had a baby, our children, aged 10 and 12 at the time, came up with the idea of gifting them an ABC poster full of impossibly long and difficult words.

But the words were too long and we had to make a book.

When the Coronavirus disrupted life as we knew it, we sheltered in place and focused on the project as a family.

This project was truly a team effort. Many of the drawings look different because they were created by different family members.

Our journey has taught us persistence, some utterly useless words, and the hard reality that we will lose money on every book we sell.

But don't let that stop you.

Special Acknowledgments:
Michelle Morkel, our fearless layout artist